BOSCASTLE

Michael Williams

BOSSINEY BOOKS

*Printed in Great Britain by
Penwell Ltd., Parkwood, Callington,
Cornwall*

PLATE ACKNOWLEDGEMENTS

Front cover photography — Ray Bishop

Back cover photography — Richard Hawken

Ray Bishop: page 17

Paul Broadhurst: pages 5, 20

J. Cork: page 26

George Ellis: page 42

Richard Hawken: page 12, 35, 36

R. Isbell: page 27

DRAWINGS

Carole Vincent: page 45

Felicity Young: pages 6, 8, 15, 41

ABOUT THE AUTHOR

A CORNISHMAN, Michael Williams started full–time publishing in 1975. With his wife Sonia, he runs Bossiney Books from a cottage and converted barn in North Cornwall— they are literally cottage publishers, specialising in Westcountry subjects by Westcountry authors. For ten years they ran the Bossiney House Hotel, just outside Tintagel—hence the name Bossiney Books.

In addition to publishing and writing, Michael Williams is a keen cricket enthusiast and collector of cricket books. He is President of the Cornish Crusaders Cricket Club and a member of the Cornwall and Gloucestershire County Clubs. He is also a member of the RSPCA, and has actively worked for reform in laws relating to animal welfare. In 1984, he was elected to the Ghost Club, and remains convinced Cornwall is the most haunted area in the whole of Great Britain.

His most recent Cornish titles are *About the Lizard* and *St Ives*. He first wrote about Boscastle in 1975, and this is an enlarged and updated version of that earlier work. He is currently writing *Secret Cornwall*.

As a publisher, he launched his first Wiltshire publications in 1989. Bossiney now covers six areas: Cornwall, Devon, Dorset, Somerset, Avon and Wiltshire.

Introducing Boscastle

N ORTH Cornwall has a glorious coastline - and Boscastle is one of its gems.

Boscastle has been known to sailors since men first sailed our British seas. Down the ages seamen and women have loved the odd little harbour here, and many of us maintain there are few finer walks in all Britain than along the cliffs from Boscastle to Tintagel.

A quarter of a century ago Ronald Duncan, farmer and poet, playwright and autobiographer, on a North Cornish expedition enthused about some of the architecture in the High Street: 'Here are a row of buildings which were designed without an architect. Nobody planned them. Use designed them, local skill built them.'

E.M. Forester once suggested the best way of exploring is to 'wander aimlessly about,' and this is probably true of Boscastle. Sonia and I have known the village for 25 years, and still rate it one of the loveliest villages in all North Cornwall - and don't neglect inland Boscastle, for there is some beautiful countryside. It was a wise Greek who said: I wanted to know, so I went to see.' We advise you to do just that.

It was here at Boscastle that Thomas Hardy wrote:
'O the opal and the sapphire of that wandering western sea
And the woman riding high above with bright hair flapping free
The woman whom I loved so, and who loyally loved me.'
All too often though, writers have mentioned Boscastle almost

The sturdy wall of Boscastle Harbour.

Boscastle Harbour
Fenny Young 83.

Sheltered between the hills, Boscastle keeps its secrets.

as an after-thought, a kind of postscript to Tintagel, and the legends around Arthur and the Court of Camelot. Such authors have been making a terrible mistake because the truth is Boscastle does not need the stuff of legends. Her history is real.

Yet there is an element of local folklore of course. Can there be such a thing as sheer myth? Are we to dismiss totally those who say they have heard ghostly bells out at sea off Forrabury? And what about those folk who say they have seen phantom boats - crews rowing silently, too silently, to an area where a vessel once perished?

Boscastle, like a beautiful woman, has many admirers - some would say too many admirers, particularly in the peak months of the holiday season. If, therefore, you can choose your dates in the calendar, my advice is come in the spring, when scent and optimism fill the air, or in the autumn, when the crowds have gone and the season colours the trees and the bracken with a special magic. That perceptive Westcountry author Lady Vyvyan once said of the Cornish atmosphere: 'It never beckons you on with unfulfilled promise. All the time it is close to you . . . a peculiar intimacy be- tween man and nature . . .'

Walking in and around Boscastle, researching and writing these sections, I have often thought of my old tutor who taught me that history comes from a Greek word meaning 'investigation'. Boscastle's past is a rich mine to re-open. Inevitably space has compelled me to be selective - and to compress. Moreover I have attempted to break from the old-fashioned guide book pattern with its mass and maze of bewildering facts and figures and num- bered walks with time of duration - little use really for the fast or the slow, the old and the very young.

Boscastle was inevitably an early destination in the tourist route of Cornwall. A North Cornwall guide, published in 1908, carries a half-page advertisement promoting The Wellington Hotel: 'High- class family and tourist hotel and coaching house - romantic scenery, bracing air, magnificent cliffs and lovely valleys.' Penally House also gets a half-page: 'High class boarding establishment - motor accommodation, private walk to the cliffs, golf links adjoin- ing.'

'Boscastle is the warmest, most sheltered, most verdant place along the north coast,' reflected the travel writer in that same 1908 guide.

Robert Stephen Hawker, Vicar of Morwenstow for 41 years, poet, author and creator of the modern Harvest Festival, in his book *Ride from Bude to Bos* saw Boscastle this way:

'Strange, striking and utterly unique is the first aspect of this vil- lage by the sea. The gorge or valley lies between two vast and pre- cipitous hills, that yawn asunder as if they had been cleft by the spells of some giant warlock of the west. As you descend the hill from the north you discover on the opposite side clusters of quaint old-fashioned houses, grotesque and gabled, that appear as if they clung together for mututal support on the slope of that perilous cliff. Between these houses, and sheer down the mountain descended, or rather 'fell' a steep and ugly road, which landed the traveller at last in a deep cut, or gash between the hills, called by strangers, in their courtesy, and by the inhabitants with an aborig- inal pride, "the Harbour".'

Robert Stephen Hawker who depicted Boscastle in his book
Ride from Bude to Bos. **The drawing is by Felicity Young,**
based on a sketch by the Earl of Carlisle in 1863.

Boscastle, the village, the surrounding countryside and the dramatic coastline all combine into a powerful magnet. For some people though the experience is too much. They come once, and never return like poor Walter de la Mare who fled from Cornwall, saying he only felt safe again when he knew the red soil of Devon was beneath his feet.

Sir John Betjeman, who knew North Cornwall well and loved it dearly, once said that the old Cornwall is now mostly to be found on foot. That is especially true in and around Boscastle: enjoy your walking.

Boscastle, as seen through the camera of Herbert Hughes
around 1905.

BOSCASTLE AND THE BARONS

YOU can approach Boscastle from several angles, by boat is probably the most romantic; but as far as land routes go, the approach from the Camelford road takes the prize. It is a glorious prospect over Valency Valley and the Atlantic Ocean; from a height of some 800 feet you suddenly burst upon the view and begin the long, twisting descent into the village.

Boscastle derives its name from Bottreaux Castle, once the old baronial residence of the Bottreaux family who held the 12 knights' fee in the county.

The Castle, alas, has vanished. You will find a narrow tarmac path leading to its site, off the old hill, below the Clovelly-like cottages and opposite the Men's Institute. Today, standing on the spot, looking across the wooded valley to the fields and the grazing cattle who look as if they are standing in the sky, it is not easy mentally to reconstruct and recapture its former significance. In the words of Sir John Maclean: 'It is situated on the sharp spur of a hill at the junction of the two valleys. On the lower, or northern side, the sites of the outer and inner walls are very distinguishable. They were of a circular form and are marked by mounds of rubbish, from which, we are informed, ashlar stones have from time to time been removed for building purposes. The defence on this side must have been strong, but what protection existed on the other sides it is not easy to discern, the site occupied by cottages and gardens. We apprehend, however, that the castle could never have offered much resistance to an enemy, being commanded by higher ground on three of its sides.'

Leland, who saw the site two centuries earlier, considered it 'far unworthie the name castel; the people there call it the court.' But Bernard S. Lowe, a one-time Rector and author of an official local guide, said: 'The castle was somewhat similar to Restormel, it could not have been so large as Launceston as some have thought. One great authority however inferred from the size of the dungeons that it must have been a castle of some importance.' Furthermore, Lowe dates the Castle as between 1080 and 1117 built 'in the usual Norman style; a keep with dwelling rooms and a wall around.' Norman Barons from Anjou, the de Bottreaux, settled in Cornwall sometime after 1066, giving their name to the parish of Minster or, as it was then called, Talkarn. The family descended from one Alan Fergant, Earl of Brittany, who was created the Earl of Richmond by William the Conqueror for his services at the Battle of Hastings; other awards being tracts of land and churches in Somerset and Cornwall.

Tantalizingly though, there are no records of any Bottreaux burials in the parish; presumably their coffins must have been carried further afield.

Tantalizingly too, there is no sign of the manor house built by John Hender soon after he had purchased the Bottreaux land from the Earl of Huntingdon in 1575. It was, it seems a grand building with wainscotted windows and a long banqueting hall, and in the days when the Cottons reigned as Lord of the Manor (1607 until 1700) it was referred to as 'the great house;' though a deed dated 1611 mentioned 'All that Mansion House called Bottreaux Castle.' But by 1814 - one year before Wellington and Waterloo - it had so declined that it was pulled down. 'The site was cut through in the making of the New Road,' said Sir John Maclean. 'Some few remains yet exist which show that it was built in the Tudor style of Architecture . . . the stables on the opposite side of the street remain though in much decay, behind which were the gardens in which there continues to grow a gigantic pear tree.' Unhappily for today's visitor there are no physical hints as to what must - in its heyday - have been the most imposing residence for miles around. It probably stood on the site of the present Bottreaux House or, at least, very near it.

Another vanished piece of Boscastle history is the Market House which was taken down in 1870. Here though there is no doubt about precise location. It stood on the ground between the Mission Hall and the New Road. Lyson, Magna Britannia, says that 'in the year 1204, William de Bottrell had a grant of a market on Wednesdays at Tolcarne; this grant was renewed in 1312 by Sir William Bottreaux, and a fair at the Festival of St. James . . .

Markets were, in fact, held here until the 1960s, and once upon a time two annual Fairs were held; Lamb Fair in early July, and Martin's Fair on November 22 and 23, when bills were settled and The Wellington bustled with celebration dinners. Credit, in some cases, stretched across the calendar. Blacksmiths, carpenters, shoemakers and doctors were all paid just once a year.

Boscastle dreams through an autumn afternoon.

CHAPEL OF ST. JAMES

MYSTERY or an unanswered question usually hovers over some chapter of local history. In the case of Boscastle it is the Chapel of St. James. Who built it? Why and when? One theory is that the line of chapels and churches down the coastline, all dedicated to St. James, rather suggests that they were on the ancient pilgrim route to Compostella in Spain. Another school of thought suggests that it may have been a private chapel of the Castle and later the Manor. But as with the Court of Camelot, we shall now never know the true answer.

But this much we do know: it stood on the site of the present Mission Hall, and, according to Sir John Maclean's researches, it was employed until about 1800. His history of *The Deanery of Trigg Minor* contains a sketch, done in 1846, showing the ruins of the tower. Apparently the bell was rung over-enthusiastically at a wedding, cracked and had to be taken down!

The chapel cemetery almost certainly stretched across part of the grounds of the Old Post House, for there is a segment of grey slate headstone, dated 1793, in the garden; and inside the house by the fireplace in the dining room is a fine old granite pillar which is thought to have come from the chapel. That attractive stone arch at Gunpool too is believed to be another legacy from St. James, as are the stone lancet windows high on the face of the present Mission Hall. Indeed one wonders just how many Boscastle homes include some relic from St. James.

In Fore Street, on the right-hand side, above the butcher's shop, stood a former Boscastle pub, The Old Boscastle Inn, which boasted a skittle alley. Now divided into two private houses, the setting still somehow manages to give an air of the Boscastle of long ago.

Rev. W.J.C. Armstrong, writing of this property in about 1930, mentioned '. . . its door well-provided with numerous bolts and bars. The door, by the way, was originally a side door straight into the street, and is said to have been so made that the smugglers might gain entrance without disturbing the inmates. Another door, now blocked up, leads into a room beyond; beyond which again is a curious low door-way, with pointed head, that might remind one of Ali Baba and the Forty Thieves, and so too the massive granite trough though, truth to tell it is but a salting trough. Upstairs the rooms are very quaint, and the floors give one the feeling of being on board ship in a heavy swell. From one of the upstairs rooms there is a charming view over the village and sea.' Sixty years on, the salting trough and the low 'door-way' with its pointed head remain.

In the last century when the flame of Methodism was burning brightly, Boscastle had as many as three chapels with a fourth at Treworld, and a fifth near the Trevalga cross-roads. Today there is only one in the village - though Trevalga remains in limited operation. Boscastle's sole surviving chapel wears a tower, and is, in fact, the oldest of the group, having been opened in 1825. You will find it in the sloping, winding Fore Street, and on an outside wall you can see the three dedications to the three now extinct chapels, words carefully shaped into grey slate, sombre reminders of Methodism's decline in the south-west. The old Wesleyan chapel of Ebenezer, further down the road, has become the village post office; the former Bible Christian Chapel of Siloam, standing at Paradise cross-roads, has been converted into a flat and garage; while Treworld is only a ruin and a memory.

A splendid factual story links wines and spirits to this present Nonconformist chapel in Fore Street. A vessel, owned by Messrs. Sloggatt and Rosevear, the Boscastle wine merchants, on a return voyage encountered a French privateer who attempted an ambush; but the Cornish captain, applying full sail, headed for his home port. The Frenchman however chased hard until both vessels were just off the entrance to Boscastle Harbour. The French captain, thinking the Cornishman was driving to destruction on the jagged rocks and not knowing the secret of the hidden harbour, sailed back to France without reward. While on land, the Boscastle wine merchants, in gratitude, contributed a sum of money for the improvement and enlargement of the teetotal chapel . . .

BOSCASTLE HARBOUR

THERE are some lovely Boscastle cottages. Real gems, planned by necessity and brought to life by native skill and craft, they shame much of modern architecture. But the principal attraction is the harbour. Quaint and picturesque may be over-worked words, yet they fit perfectly in this case.

Times were when Boscastle was a busy port, dealing with 100-ton vessels that were towed in by men in rowing boats, aided by horses on the tow paths. The horses were housed in the Palace stables - now the site of the Youth Hostel - and they would have been shod at the old forge, a stone building with wooden shutters which today is an information centre and shop for the National Trust, standing by Valency Row. Wine and spirits, beer and bricks, coal and manure, groceries and timber all arrived by ship; and traffic was two-way in that the same vessels took away Cornish minerals and slate, china clay and corn. As many as 200 ships put in here in the space of a year; and one resident recalled seeing 13 in the harbour at the same time. But the coming of the railway to Camelford in August 1893 altered all that.

It is an unusual harbour: a medieval breakwater, a long, grey slipway and huge dog–leg opening into the ocean, tucked inland nearly out of sight of the sea

Felicity Young.

Boscastle Harbour.

Cottages, rushing water, a tiny bridge—a cameo from artist Felicity Young.

– as the French privateer discovered. Sir Richard Grenville of *Revenge* fame built the jetty back in 1584. Almost opposite the jetty is the outer bar.

It was in the year 1536 that John Leland referred to Boscastle as 'a pore Havenet of no certaine Salvegarde,' and in the 1580s Sir Richard Grenville, then High Sheriff of Cornwall, commanded the rebuilding of the quay. The outer breakwater was an addition in 1820, but it was destroyed by a mine during the last war and then reconstructed by the National Trust in 1962 with stone from the old Laira Bridge across the Tamar in Plymouth.

Cliffs of slate and shale tower impressively, somehow giving the impression of reluctance, a reluctance to admit the Atlantic or let loose the waters of the Valency and the Jordan. The two rivers converge at Boscastle, '. . . and so do two geological formations,' wrote Sir John Betjeman, the Poet Laureate, in his Shell Guide *Cornwall*. 'The northern half marks the beginning of that rather uneventful clayey country associated with parishes like Week St. Mary, which is characteristic of northernmost Cornwall and North Devon where 'The hammer of the south west wind smites on the anvil of the yellow clay.' The southern part, which is the border of Forrabury parish, is the beginning of the slate and granite of the rest of Cornwall.'

If you are at Boscastle an hour before low tide, make sure you see and hear the blow hole which throws a cloud of white spray cascading with an astonishingly loud report across the harbour. One novelist, in an imaginative moment, christened it 'The Devil's Bellows.' It is positioned below Profile Rock, whose features, from certain angles, uncannily resemble Queen Victoria.

Profile Rock.

Cecil Williamson with some of his collection.

WITCHCRAFT MUSEUM

CORNWALL - or parts of her - has a supernatural quality.
The lonely moors, the derelict mines, the dark woods, an isolated cottage or manor house - all these can have a haunted and haunting atmosphere. Who would connect the black arts and Boscastle? Yet here, by the water's edge, you will find a witchcraft museum. Formerly a mineral store and shipping warehouse, Cecil Williamson has gathered together a fascinating collection.

Grotesque headmasks, a bottle of witch's brew, the skin of a snake used as a warlock's belt or a witch's garter, two witch's trumpets made from human thigh bones used for calling up the spirits of the dead, instruments of African witch doctors - these are only a handful of the exhibits. There is even the skeleton of a witch, lying in an open elm coffin. The iron spikes, lying alongside, were driven through her body in an attempt to hold her down in her grave and to prevent her from haunting.

'There are basically four aspects of magical operation,' explains Cecil Williamson. 'First, you have the source of the elemental spirit force; secondly, you have the witch; thirdly, you have the client; and fourthly, the objective. Witchcraft's a very private, a very personal service. Each case calls for considerable expenditure of time and energy. It also calls for considerable expenditure in the other sense. A witch expects payment; on occasions very large sums of money pass hands. The rituals themselves are elaborate, long incantations, a secret language is spoken: a mumbo-jumbo of gibberish·sounds . . . ill-wishing's principally through a powerful prayer, a projection of thoughts to the exclusion of all else throughout the operation. While there's hate, envy, greed, lust and jealousy in the world, the witch won't be short of clients.'

THE SHIP AND HAWKER

ONCE upon a time Boscastle had as many as 18 pubs or ale houses, one such establishment was The Ship in Valency Row, near the harbour, now a private residence and re-named The Old Ship. Robert Stephen Hawker, as a young undergraduate, sampled its hospitality, recalling:

'We reached in safety our bourn for the night at the bottom of the hill, and discovered the hostelry by the sign which swung above the door. This appeared to us to represent a man's shoe; but when we read the legend, we found that it signified The Ship Inn, and was the 'actual effigy' of a vessel which belonged to the port. Here we received a smiling welcome from the hostess, a ruddy-visaged widow. She then invited us to enter her 'parrolar,' a room rather cosy than magnificent; for when our landlady had followed in her two guests, and stood at the door, no one beside could have forced an entrance any more than a cannon ball could cleave through a feather-bed. We then proceeded to confer about beds for the night and not without misgivings, inquired if she could supply a couple of those indispensable places of repose. A demur ensued. All the gentry in the town, she declared, were accustomed to sleep 'two in a bed,' and the officers that travelled the country, and stopped at her house, would mostly do the same; but however if we commanded two beds for only two people, two we must have; only, although they were in the same room, we must certainly pay for two, sixpence apiece was her regular price. We assented, and then went on to entreat that we might dine. She graciously agreed; but to all our questions as to fare, her sole response was 'Meat – meat and taties. Some call 'em,' she added in a scornful tone, 'putraties, but we always say taties here.' The specific difference beef, mutton, veal, etc., seemed to be utterly or artfully ignored, and to every frenzied inquiry her calm, inexorable reply was 'Meat – nice wholesome meat and taties.'

'It is a wretched truth that by no effort could we ascertain what

Colonel Hawker's Green Cut provides a pleasant stroll.

it was roasted for us by Widow Treworgy, hostess of The Ship, and which we consumed. Was it a Boscastle baby? There was not a vestige of bone nor any outline that we could identify the joint, and the not unsavoury taste was something like tender veal. It was not until years afterwards that light was thrown on our mysterious dinner that day by a passage which I accidentally turned up in an ancient history of Cornwall. Therein I read that 'the sillie people of Bouscastle and Boussiney do catch in the summer seas divers young soleys (seals), which, doubtful if they be fish or flesh, convynge housewives will nevertheless roast, and do make thereof very savoury meat.' The bill which we duly transcribed ran:

Captens

T for 2 0	6
Sleep for 2 1	0
Meat & Taties & Bier 1	6
Breasks 1	6

There is an interesting little postscript to The Ship story. Apparently the atmosphere that night was so stuffy that neither Hawker nor his colleague could sleep, so they dressed early and went out to explore Boscastle at first light. Discovering that nearly every cottage had its own pigsty, they let loose all the pigs in the village!

Hawker grew into one of the most talked-about parsons in the kingdom. His exploits coping with ship-wrecked sailors made him a living legend. A talented several-sided character - poet, creator of the modern Harvest Festival service, and architect of that remarkable Rectory at Morwenstow - he was a regular visitor to Penally House. The present residence, white-faced and late Regency, was built by the merchant William Sloggatt in 1836. It stands in its own grounds high above the outgoing road to Bude. Here Hawker stayed with his brother Claude, Sloggatt's son-in-law. In fact some of his last days in Cornwall were spent at Penally in June, 1875, when Claude described him as 'very ill and certainly broken in his mind.' By the end of August, Robert Stephen Hawker was in his grave, incredibly not in his beloved Morwenstow churchyard but in a Plymouth cemetery, and even more incredibly an alleged death-bed convert to the Roman Catholic Church: an earthly end shrouded in controversy.

Some people have suggested that a tunnel leads from Penally House to the sea - a smuggler's avenue – but, to date, nothing has been found. Intriguingly though the house is minus a cellar. There is, too, a ghostly reputation and more than one person has claimed to have heard unaccountable footsteps.

The green cut, ironically known as the private road, connecting Penally House and Penally Terrace - ironically because there is a public right of way - was created by Colonel Hawker. It seems that he clashed badly with the agent for the harbour and planned to avoid using the harbour roads, but on completion of his 'private road' to facilitate unloading goods at his warehouse, now The Cobweb, he encountered yet another legal hurdle. And life became so difficult that he committed suicide; so for the Hawker brothers there was no happy ending.

However, you can today stroll along the once controversial green cut, getting as you go, a bird's eye view of part of the village.

MANOR ESTATE

BOSCASTLE village and the neighbouring countryside are comparatively unscarred. A major factor in its preservation is the fact that Boscastle for many years was a Manor Estate.

It was last sold as such in 1946. In the words of the auctioneers, Kivell and Sons: 'In the rural areas of Camelford and mainly in the Ecclesiastical Parish of Minster and Forrabury, with certain outlying portions in Lesnewth, St. Juliot and Trevalga . . . Boscastle Manor Estate comprising the greater part of the unspoilt, old-world town of Boscastle and surrounding countryside, including: Residences, Boarding Houses, Commercial Premises, The Wellington Hotel and The Napoleon Inn, Farms, Small Holdings, Cottages, Accommodation Lands and choice Building Sites, the Harbour, Cliffs, Woodlands, etc., as tenanted and some $1^{1}/_{2}$ miles of the River Valency.' About 1,450 acres, the Estate was offered as a whole or in 144 lots.

A sale was scheduled to be held on Friday, September 20, 1946, at the Public Hall - later Piper's Cafe by the harbour - but matters never reached that fateful Friday, for the Manor Estate was bought privately for £90,000 by Thomas Percy Fulford, a wealthy agricultural merchant living at Launceston. But his reign as the last Lord of the Manor was brief, for within a matter of months he was selling individual properties. The previous year, T.P. (as he was known to his friends) had stood as Conservative candidate for North Cornwall in a three-cornered General Election, when he polled 16,171 votes, going under by 2,655 to the Liberal, T.L. Horabin.

THE HOSTELRIES

DRINKING in Boscastle may not have declined, but those 18 ale houses have shrunk to three fully licensed premises.

At the top of the hill, below quaintly named Paradise, is The Napoleon, an attractive white-faced 16th century inn with an eye-catching sign showing Napoleon riding his grey horse Marengo across the Alps. Boscastle tradition declares that the inn was used as a recruiting office during the Napoleonic wars, and the landlord himself joined Wellington's ranks to go to Waterloo. On returning to North Cornwall he was nicknamed the Napoleon man and consequently christened his inn accordingly. Should you be contemplating a visit to 'The Nap,' as it is known locally, make sure you see Boney's bar, a delightful little section of the inn decorated with prints from the life and times of the French General.

Nothing personifies Cornish rivalry better than the fact that the hotel downalong, at the foot of the Old Road, is named the Wellington. Originally known at The Bos Castle Hotel, it was re-

The Napoleon Inn.

named Scott's Wellington on the Duke's death in 1852 - an interesting choice in view of the Iron Duke's belief that the British Army was recruited 'from the dregs of society . . . they have all enlisted for the drink!' There is a touch of irony, too, about their respective geographies with Napoleon, despite defeat at Waterloo, lording it at the top of the hill while the victorious Wellington stands at the bottom.

One of the oldest coaching inns along this North Cornish coast, The Wellington is more than three centuries old; indeed parts of the building go back to four centuries. Boscastle, in fact, depended on horse-drawn coaches until the early 1920s which makes The Wellington one of the last posting houses in Britain. A number of present day residents can readily recall the coachman's horn, the clatter of hooves and the clink of harness as the coach rumbled down Fore Street, into Dunn Street and the Old Hill, depositing passengers in the yard.

An advertisement in *The Plymouth, Devonport and Stonehouse Herald*, dated July 29, 1849, read: 'The Albion Omnibus, with first-rate horses and driver, leaves Saltash every Wednesday at ten o'clock precisely, passes Callington, and reaches Five Lanes at twenty past three, where it remains for one hour, and finally reaches Boscastle with Mail Coach regularity at seven o'clock. Fares, whole distances, 4s 6d inside, 3s 4½d outside.'

Substantially rebuilt in 1853 to cope with the increased number of travellers, The Wellington today is a scheduled historic building. If you pay a visit, try to see the exquisite hanging oil lamps, which originally hung in St. Juliot Church, installed by Hardy himself. Other interesting features are the collection of etchings and prints concerning the Duke of Wellington, and the four stained glass windows in the long bar - these came from another Cornish coaching inn, Olivers' Royal Hotel at Bodmin. They were made in 1846 to commemorate Queen Victoria's visit to the county town, each window being in the shape of a quarter of the Royal Standard.

Unfortunately there is no evidence to indicate a visit by the General 'with his hooked nose and piercing eye.' But in the 1870s a royal party stayed at the hotel which, it is believed, included Edward VII and a lady friend.

Another eminent visitor in the last century was Sir Henry Irving, the first actor to be knighted. Somerset-born, Irving spent most of his childhood in West Cornwall, and later in an interview with Sir Arthur Quiller-Couch, attributed his stamina to 'the free and open and healthy years' he had enjoyed in the south-west. A chair, used by Irving in some of his London productions, was made from woodwork of Minster Church during its restoration when timber changed hands for less than £1 a ton. Irving was greatly interested in the reputed magical powers of a certain Boscastle woman - believed to be a witch - so much so that he gave her an allowance, paid quarterly by the wife of the Boscastle doctor. A string of misfortunes robbed the famous actor-manager of most of his money in the 1890s, and it is possible that he may have been hoping to use her powers to unwind the bad spell.

The Cobweb is Boscastle's youngest public house. In 1945 its life style changed from a store and two years later it acquired a full licence. The building dating from the late 1600s, was an off-licence from somewhere in the 1700s and, for a good many years, it was Sloggatt's warehouse and office. The crook for a pulley is a reminder of the days when corn and grain were lifted to the top floor

For generations one bar was festooned with cobwebs, but cob-

Coach and four outside the Wellington in 1913.

webs and spiders have long since departed. When wine and spirits were housed in this section of the store, the merchants believed the cobwebs helped to keep flies away from the casks, and anyone removing them was destined for instant dismissal. Two interesting items are a sheep or goat bell from Trevalga and a wooden rattle, not to cheer on Boscastle football team, but to scare away the crows; and in the next room you can see a set of eight brass rum measures, the largest of which holds four gallons.

But the most interesting article is a finely carved figure-head behind the cobwebbed bar. It came from a Swedish ship called *The Welm* which perished in a fierce gale on Black Rock, a few miles up the coast near Crackington Haven, about 1890. Despite valiant rescue attempts, only one member of the crew - the mate - was saved. This, and other brave rescue attempts made locally, would seem to reinforce the view that though smuggling was acceptable, wrecking was not.

THOMAS HARDY & ST. JULIOT

YOU can still enjoy the walk up Valency Valley from the wooden gates at the entrance to the meadows, above the public car park opposite The Cobweb. Pylons excepted, it is almost unchanged since Thomas Hardy walked it a century ago. There is a hint of

The Cobweb Inn, the regulars, including dog—and authentic cobwebs.

Water tumbles over the falls in the Valency Valley.

Exmoor in places, and the path upward through Minster Woods to Minster Church is especially lovely in spring or in the autumn when the leaves turn copper, fall and fade away.

High on the northern shoulder of this broad valley stands the Church of St. Julitta, the reason why Hardy, then a young architect, came to Cornwall in 1872. He was brought to St. Juliot to assist in its restoration, arriving at the Rectory on a Monday evening in March, wearing a grubby raincoat with a recently written poem sticking out of his pocket. A fateful evening it proved too, for he was received by Emma Lavinia Gifford, sister-in-law of the Rev. Caddell Holder, the incumbent: a woman of 29 with corn-coloured hair who, four years later, became Mrs Thomas Hardy.

Though no beauty, Emma Gifford could be vivacious, rode well and was genuinely interested in literature. In a manuscript discovered after her death, she recalled their romance: 'My architect came two or three times a year . . . I rode my pretty mare Fanny, and he walked by my side, and I showed him more of the neighbourhood - the cliffs along the roads, and through the scattered hamlets, sometimes gazing down at the small solemn shores below, where seals lived, coming out of the great deep caverns occasionally . . . often we walked to Boscastle down the beautiful Valency Valley where we would jump over a low wall by rough steps or get through a narrow footpath to come out on to great wide spaces suddenly, with a little brook going the same way, in which we once lost a tiny picnic tumbler, and there it is to this day no doubt between two of the boulders' (An incident which Hardy used in his poem *Under the Waterfall*).

'Sometimes we drove to Tintagel and Trebarwith Strand, where donkeys were employed carrying seaweed to the farmers; Strangles Beach, also Bossiney, Bude and other places along the coast. Lovely drives they were, with sea views all along at intervals . . .'

Thankfully those sea views remain. Hardy, of course, if he came back tomorrow, would inevitably see some development, and would find our main roads crowded at the height of the holiday season.

Unhappily, the Hardy's marriage turned sour. Hardy himself was a lugubrious spirit; as one critic put it, his stories are 'more often November than May.' But equally he had great personal problems with Emma, who grew into an exceedingly difficult woman, possibly even slightly mad. A snob to the extent of telling him in public that he had married a lady, she attempted to get his book *Jude the Obscure* banned on the grounds of obscenity. In the words of one literary gossip: 'her whole bitter purpose was to belittle, irritate and discourage her husband.' For more than 30 years they existed in a state of disharmony, Emma, for some years banishing herself to an uncomfortable attic.

And yet incredibly after her death in 1912 Hardy, looking back on their earlier romance, came back to Cornwall: a return that triggered some of his most moving work, probably some of the greatest love poems ever written. Writing about his departed wife became nearly a post mortem obsession:

'What if still in chasmal beauty looms the wild weird western
          shore,
The woman now is elsewhere whom that ambling pony bore,
And knows nor cares for Beeny, and will laugh there never
more.'

Boscastle is, in fact, the Castle Boterel in his novel *A Pair of Blue Eyes*, the story of a young architect coming to Endelstow in North Cornwall in connection with a church restoration, a romance that ends with the lovers travelling on the same train, one a corpse inside a coffin.

Hardy, like others in the literary field, was fascinated by the ruins of Tintagel Castle. In those early happy days, the lovers lingered so long on one occasion that they were locked in and only avoided a night's 'imprisonment' by frantically waving their handkerchiefs to the cottagers in the cove.

In 1916, with the Great War raging, Hardy brought his second wife to North Cornwall, and there was a sad little episode at Tintagel Church. Thinking they had not been warmly received, they marched out as the Vicar began his sermon. The Hardys had apparently tried to sit on the old stone bench in the south transept – the nave presumably being packed – Hardy wanting a full-length view of the nave so as to compare the changes since Emma had done her painting years before.

He never came back.

As for St. Juliot and the present, Hardy has left some of the work of the 15th century masons for you to see: the embattled porch with its stone roof and carved wall plates, the splendid arcade, and the granite font in which babies were baptised five centuries ago - these are their legacies. There are two tablets commemorating the Hardy association and copies of sketches by the young architect. Emma conducted the choir here and played the harmonium. The tower, with battlements and pinnacles but minus buttresses, is Hardy's creation; Emma herself laid the first stone.

Up the twisting lane stands the Rectory, now a private house and not on view to the public. A slate-fronted building with French windows, it was built in 1851 with stone from the nearby quarry. It overlooks a peaceful sloping garden, punctuated with trees. Hardy's seat, facing south to south-east, is still in the garden; it was here that he proposed to Emma. Also nearby is the old St. Juliot Church Day School, the pupils of which attended the ceremony when Emma laid a foundation stone at the church, when the Vicar urged the children to remember the occasion and pass on its details to their children and grandchildren.

CAROLE VINCENT

MOST of Cornwall's important creative characters in the arts have tended to operate at the western end of Cornwall.

But Boscastle can proudly boast one such creative personality in Carole Vincent. She is an all-rounder; though principally known for her sculptures, she also paints in oils, gouache and watercolours.

'I came to Boscastle in 1961 for six months, a teaching supply post, liked the place and have been here ever since!' 1988 was an important cross-roads in her life: her construction of the controversial giant sun- dial in the commercial heart of Plymouth. The dial makes an exciting focal point for thousands of people in the city, but, at the time, it had its critics. Miss Vincent philosophically reflects: 'The truth is there's no such thing as bad publicity.'

Like that great sculptor of St Ives, Dame Barbara Hepworth, Carole Vincent enjoys living and working in Cornwall, often finding impressive compelling sculptural inspiration in the Cornish landscape. Born in Crediton, Devon, Carole recently had another prestigious commission: in 1989 she was asked to create a work for Devon County Council to mark the Year of the Pedestrian. 'The Devon Pedestrians' are now in Exeter, Torquay, Barnstaple and Plymouth, but you can see a copy of the group standing in her garden at Half Acre, a grand old stone cottage with her studio, which is really a multi-purpose workshop, alongside. Here she holds classes for painters and sculptors, the young and the old, the amateur and the accomplished. North Cornwall, and Boscastle in particular, owes a special debt to Carole Vincent for her own con- siderable contribution to the arts scene - and for her encouragement of others.

Painter and sculptor Carole Vincent who finds her inspiration in the Boscastle landscape.

MINSTER

MINSTER is the Mother Church of Boscastle.

Whether you approach it from the climbing path through Minster Woods or via the lane linking Boscastle and Lesnewth, it comes as a delightful surprise. Set in an amphitheatre of trees, stately ivy-coated ashes and sycamores, the setting is almost too pretty to be true, particularly in the spring when daffodils and bluebells splash their colours over the old churchyard. And a surprise in that the saddleback tower appears unexpectedly below the level of the land. There is no hamlet of Minster, not a house in sight, the last place that you might expect to find a Church. Actually the daffodils were the brain child of the Rev. Bernard Lowe, who had the seeds sown during the Great War. An enterprising cleric, he wrote and published penny books of prayer that were read all over the country.

This was another North Cornish church that fired the poetic imagination of Hawker:

> 'Sadly are these walls; the cloister lowly laid
> Where passing monks at solemn evening made their
> chanted orisons.'

Originally, Minster was known as Tolcarne or Talkarn, meaning rock chapel or cell. A priory was created here by William, son of Nicholas Boterel (or Bottreaux) which was handed over to the monks of St. Sergius in Anjou and, in time, it became a cell of that French priory; the site of the priory being slightly below the church on the northern side. A Holy Well is also in the churchyard.

Time, however, took heavy toll of Minster, and by 1868 - the year that Gladstone first became Prime Minister - it had sunk into tragic decay, so much so that the roof fell in shortly after Matins one Sunday. But thanks to the generosity of Miss Helyar, Patron of the Living, the nave, aisle and tower were restored and the church re-opened on January 4, 1871.

There are several items worth noting here at Minster. On the wall of the chancel you will see the black and white figures of William Cotton and his wife and their eight children. It has been suggested that this inscription inspired those famous lines by Sir Henry Wootton:

'She first deceased him; he a little tried
To live without her; liked it not, and died'.

Two other interesting graves in corners of the church concern Sir John Cotton, a 17th century knight, and his servant Nicholas Tooker who, in the inscription, calls across the church:

'A greater master calls, dear sir adieu:
I always thought to live and die with you'.

And on the south wall you'll find John Hender and his wife, kneeling at a desk, wearing the ruffles of Shakespeare's fashion, while in the north wall you will detect the faint outline of an original door. Minster has this power to pull us back into history. There is that ten inch brass on the end of the south wall of the chancel, commemorating the death of a child, Hender Robartes, who passed away just before Elizabeth I. The Norman font, too, is interesting in that its basket-work ornament closely resembles that at Forrabury and, oddly enough, a pillar in Durham Cathedral. There is also a Jacobean table with chalice-like legs, thought to have been employed as an altar, and the Crucifix on the rood- beam has come a long way, for it was carved in Oberammergau. One window has 16th century glass and bears the arms of that famous Cornish family, the Trelawneys.

But most intriguing of all is the pair of scissors carved halfway up the western face of the tower. These are an unsolved mystery - nobody knows their origin or purpose.

The walls and pews of this old church badly need repair; therefore any donation, large or small, is welcome. Indeed this is true of nearly all our country churches. The struggle against decay is constant.

The lane from Minster to Lesnewth had been called 'sylvan' by Sir John Betjeman. City motorists may be less polite! And herein lies the joy of it: twisting and turning, rising and plunging, forever narrow; most motorists avoid it. It takes you through the little hamlet of Treworld and, at points, crosses streams. At any time of the year it remains one of the most pleasant walks in all North Cornwall.

LESNEWTH

LESNEWTH stands at the head of a quiet wooded valley, quiet unless the wind stirs and starts muttering among the trees. Like Minster, this Church of St. Michael and All Angels was built in a dip. Prior to Norman times, it was a custom to build churches inland in the hope of avoiding Scandinavian invaders; we therefore find these older churches strategically tucked away in the countryside and the later buildings, after the Norman Conquest, occupying more exposed positions by the coast.

The word Lesnewth means new court, and was possibly so-called when it became the capital of a sub-division of the ancient Hundred of Trigg in Saxon days. Again, like Minster, there are links across the Channel. A member of the Pomeroy family gave the right of appointing a Rectory to the Abbey of Val in Normandy which, in 1237, sold it to Henry de Daneys, reserving a princely pension of five shillings. It is believed that the first church was erected by the Saxons. Despite its cleverly concealed geography, the church had the ill-luck to be spotted by marauding Danes who pillaged it on their way to sack Manor Helsey.

The second church, built by the Normans, was cruciform in shape. Again like neighbouring Minster, it fell into depressing dilapidation, and in 1862 the ruthless J.P. St. Aubyn presided over its restoration. Parts of the original incorporated into the present building are the three-pointed doorway and a Norman altar slab over the sill of the north window in the chancel. Dynamite was used in the demolition, and fragments of the old church can be seen sunken into the hedge, south west of the tower. Lesnewth, like so many North Cornish churches, suffered badly from drastic restoration. The restorers, in their enthusiasm, destroyed so many good things, but few people regretted the disappearance of the old- fashioned pew boxes.

In this context, A.J. Beresford Hope, M.P., told an amusing story at the re-opening of Lesnewth in 1866. '. . . a church having been restored, where the Squire of the Parish thinking himself a fine fellow, said the church was good enough for farmers and shop-keepers, and he would not have his gallery taken down. The church was restored in a very beautiful manner, only that abominable cage in which the Squire sat was retained. When the church was opened, the Squire, who thought he had done a very

34

Minster—majestic, hidden and full of history.

clever thing, went up to the principal farmer saying '. . . Mr Jones, you see I have stuck to my old pew; what do people say of me?' Jones scratched his head and repeated the question . . . "Well, sir, if you will have me to tell you, they say you look like a jackass in a horsebox!"

Outside, standing above the stream which passes through the churchyard and near the white railed footbridge is another good example of a Celtic cross. This one is said to have stood originally at Waterpit Down. A curate suggested that it should be resurrected here, but a local farmer, on whose land it had lain for some time, thought otherwise. He wanted to use it as a pig's trough.

The coastguard look–out point at Willapark.

PENTARGUN

ASSUMING that you are leaving some of the best of the Boscastle area until the last, then you would be advised to return to the coast, for the walk from the harbour to Penally Hill and on to Pentargun certainly belongs to that category.

Penally, crowned by its white flag pole, stands to the right of the har bour. The view from the summit, weather permitting, can be memorable. To the left you have a splendid foreshortened view of

36

the coast, that tortuous harbour, the rocky shape of Meachard, towering Willapark, capped by the white coastguard look-out, and beyond it the sea and the sky and the rocks all combine in drawing your eye towards Bossiney.

To the right lies the rock-bound inlet of Pentargun and Fire Beacon Point; further up the coast the serrated contours of Cambeak, that big bold headland by Crackington; and, provided the visibility is sharp, the promontory of Hartland and, with luck, Lundy Island, some 33 miles over the sea. The rocks hereabouts are dark; the cliffs inaccessible. Once more Hawker's words about a watery grave ring true, especially on a stormy day when hundreds of white horses come careering in off a heaving grey Atlantic.

At the head of the bay is a deep chasm where a stream - streamlet may be a better word - flows out from the cliff: a ribbon of cold, usually clear moorland water falling a matter of 120 feet. After heavy rain, when the chasm is filled, the spectacle can be impressive. From the rugged grandstand of the cliffs, Pentargun looks best when the tide is in, but if you want to see the waterfall and caves, coincide your visit with low tide. Pentargun has a big, echoing cave, burrowing into the cliff-face to the north. More than 200 feet in depth, it is aptly named Double Doors, for its entrance is framed by twin rock portals.

This cliffscape is fascinating yet awesome, demanding respect. Rock climbing, for example, should be left to the experts, or attempted only under their tuition. All too often a summer is darkened by some tragedy, caused by underestimating nature.

Ruth Manning-Sanders, on a twilight walk along the cliffs at Land's End, once wrote of 'the sense of the primordial, the strange and the savage, the unknown, the very long ago.' The same spirit breathes on these cliffs. In a sense they epitomise North Cornwall, somehow merging past and present, and speaking a defiant language that not even the strongest gale can silence.

Stand here, say when the sun slips westward, and you can feel close to the beginning of things - perhaps even close to the secret of Life itself.

J.M.W. Turner, greatest of all English painters, quite possibly stood here. He spent a winter in Cornwall, and there is a famous picture of Boscastle harbour depicted dramatically in a storm. Thomas Rowlandson, too, almost certainly looked out on this same Atlantic seascape. It was the London-born Rowlandson who really started the painting invasion of Cornwall. He stayed at Hengar, with the Onslow family, in that quiet inland parish off the Camelford to Bodmin road. Cornwall's magnetism for the painter cannot be merely defined as the brilliance of the light and the beauty of the place. In the words of author Denys Val Baker, it is 'a mixture of material and mystical, facts and fantasies, all equally important.' In a sentence, more has been written and painted and created here than anywhere outside London - a fascinating, almost unanswerable fact.

On the other side of the harbour is Willapark. On the map Boscastle's Willapark resembles a defiant bulldog's head, facing the Atlantic. There are marvellous views, and Sir John Maclean, visiting in 1872, gave a clue to its ancient past.

'The only work of antiquity which we have been able to discover in the ancient parishes of Forrabury and Minster is the small earthwork on Willapark Point, north of Forrabury Church. Willapark Point is a peninsula of high land jutting out into the ocean. The cliffs on every side, except for the isthmus, are very lofty, and in some places drop perpendicularly into the sea at a height of several hundred feet. The isthmus is bounded by two cavernous bays, called 'Black Pits,' of truly awful aspect; and on the eastern side, which slopes slightly down towards the abyss, are the remains of an earthwork, consisting of a wall with an eternal ditch. It does not appear to have been completed, and we may imagine that whilst in the course of preparation the threatened danger passed away, or the anticipated attack was made and, consequently, the work was either abandoned or interrupted.'

A member of the Royal Archaeological Institute of Great Britain and Ireland and Honorary Member of the Royal Institution of Cornwall, Sir John Maclean spent several weeks at a house called Riverside by the River Valency, researching into Boscastle history, basing his philosophy on the words of Camden: 'If there be any who desire to be strangers in their own country, foreigners in their own cities, and always children in knowledge, let them please themselves. I write not for such humours.'

In this dramatic setting, even a man-made construction like the white Board of Trade look-out - later used by the coastguards in an emergency - has a beckoning, compelling quality. The coastal walk towards Trevalga takes you past four disused quarries, long silent, save for the cry of birds, the wind and sea. The descent of Blackapit is steep, with chasm below, as one walker put it 'terrible, a yawning rent in the rocks, black and forbidding.'

FORRABURY

INLAND to the main road, walking across Forrabury Common, you are in a real sense walking across an edge of history. For this area is a rare relic of Celtic tenure of land; the land being divided into strips called 'stitches,' separated by little bands. They are still cultivated by North Cornish farmers who hold the rights from Lady Day to Michaelmas, and outside these dates the land becomes common grazing.

Forrabury Church, with its sturdy embattled tower, has a weather-beaten air. But inside it is something of a disappointment. It was drastically renovated around 1868. Apart from the Norman font, a Norman segment of the south wall and some old woodwork, there is little to show of its age and history. The woodwork portrays a special animal interest: pictures of a cock and hen, swans on the Jacobean pulpit, together with an ape on a stool and some rather strange rabbits. Unusually too the altar, the pulpit and the credence table have all been made from former pew ends. South of the churchyard gate, by the side road that slopes down into Boscastle, is another fine old cross, just one inch shorter than its neighbour at Trevalga. The three holes, according to local opinion, are confirmation that the cross was once used as a gatepost.

It was Forrabury that inspired Robert Stephen Hawker's dramatic poem *The Silent Tower of Bottreaux*. The verses tell that a ship was carrying bells for the church and the voyage was all but over when the pilot called out 'Thank God for a safe passage!' But the captain disagreed, saying 'Thank God on land; but at sea thank the captain and a good ship.' Whereupon a storm erupted, and ship, captain, crew and bells all perished, except the pious pilot, the only man to reach the rocky shore. It is a good story, but we have Hawker's word for it that the events were creations of his imagination. 'On the very slight ground of local suggestion, I did invent the ballad . . . if any man should suppose them to be historic or claim them for his own use, I must counter him in the phrase of Jack Cade, 'He lies, for I invented them myself!'

WELLTOWN MANOR

QUITE the loveliest house in the parish is Welltown Manor on the western boundary, just off the Tintagel to Boscastle road. An Elizabethan dwelling with mullioned windows, facing north east, it was built around 1550. A yeoman farmer, Baldwin Tinke, is thought to have been its first owner and occupant. The initials B.T. carved on the drop ends of the hood-moulding over the front door are presumed to be his.

Nine decades ago, a visitor described it as 'a small old picturesque house now in a very dilapidated condition.' Fortunately the dilapidated part can be forgotten, for inside it has been restored with pride and sensitivity: the stone circular staircase remains, as do many aged beams, one believed to have been the mast of a sailing ship, and some impressive stone-work, including two beautiful fireplaces.

In 1608, on John Tinke's death, the manor passed to his sons Baldwin and John (possibly grandsons of the original owner), but an argument developed, and the younger, thinking he had been badly treated, appealed to the Lord Chancellor who ruled that the property should be divided two thirds to the elder son and one third to the younger. It is intriguing to guess how such an arrangement worked in practice. Was the door to the dining room created for this purpose? Intriguing too is the will concerning five daughters who, on their marriage, were to be given either a lamb each or two shillings and sixpence. Which did they choose?

Set in pleasant, secluded grounds, Welltown Manor still manages to generate an aura of the past and more leisurely days. Not surprisingly that great Westcountry character Sabine Baring-Gould, author of *Onward Christian Soldiers*, and for so long squire and parson at Lewtrenchard on the English side of the Devon-Cornwall border, used it as the setting for scenes in his novel *John Herring*. Not surprisingly too there is a sunken pathway and a smuggling tradition. In such an atmosphere the imagination stirs.

But you must be warned: Welltown Manor today is a family home and not open to the public.

Wellington and Boscastle are connected in name only, there is no record that the Iron Duke ever visited the town.

For Thomas Hardy, however, Boscastle was the romantic backdrop to his life.

St Juliot Church—Hardy's link with Boscastle.

TREVALGA

FURTHER along the B3263 are cross-roads, a red Victorian post-box (note how the Victorian crown differs from those of George VI and Elizabeth II), and the hamlet of Trevalga, a name unchanged since Domesday. This hamlet is a gem: an unspoilt corner of North Cornwall. There are just two farms, a church and a handful of cottages, one of which boasts a roof almost as weird and wonderful as that capping Tintagel Post Office. The literary J.D. Cook, who was born at Camelford and is remembered in Tintagel Church, lived at Trevalga. The real joy of the place is that a former Lord of the Manor handed it over to his old school Marlborough. So as long as public schools survive, Trevalga will be safe from the developers.

The church, dedicated to St. Petroc, stands more or less in a farm yard. But the Saint would not have minded, for he was a true Celt, being half Welsh and half Irish and understanding country life. The building itself is interesting in that there are traces of Norman work in the lower masonry. The battlemented tower protecting three bells is 13th century. One of those bells sent peals across the parish for five centuries. Sadly they are now silent and will remain so unless a legacy comes their way and safety is restored. The narrow nave has a tiny chapel reached by a Norman arch, and the font was shaped by a Norman craftsman out of local greenstone. There is a piscina, a stone basin used for rinsing the chalice, and a peephole which enabled people sitting in the side chapel to see the action at the altar.

If you are interested in church art, there is plenty to see here. There is a fascinating Dutch carving in the dark wood with scenes depicting the Visitation, the Annunciation and the Crucifixion. As many as 20 characters people the three panels: Mary, seen under a canopy speaking to Gabriel, and God despatching a dove from the sky. While behind the figures of Mary and Elizabeth are two charming Dutch houses; and in the Crucifixion section John, in company with the two Marys, is seen at the foot of the cross. Four angels hold chalices at the nailed feet and hands.

There is some really noble woodwork in this building, much of it given by Bolitho Stephens in his time as Lord of the Manor. The pulpit, shaped by Exeter carvers, is to his memory, as are the sanctuary chair and desk, all of which were donated by his widow in November, 1929. The pulpit shows chapters in the career of St. Petroc who founded the monastery at Bodmin, the religious capital of the county in the Middle Ages. Notice the Saint with his stag, and with his sheepskin and staff protected by a wolf; again an angel awakes him with the command to go to Brittany. In the small panels is an especially delicate carving of a ship fully rigged. There is, too, an east window with pictures of the Adoration of the Kings, the Annunciation and the Ascension. Arthur Mee was not exaggerating when he said 'Trevalga has still an art gallery worth looking at.'

Outside in the churchyard there is an aged moss-coated cross, standing some five feet and eight inches; and, of course, there are superlative views of the Atlantic and the cliffs merging into a memorable picture.

A lane leads from the hamlet out to a strange 'terrace' of heather- peppered cliffs. If you have walked from Tintagel over the cliffs to Boscastle, you will know that words can convey only a fraction of the drama and beauty. If you have not, then you have missed a rich experience, for hereabouts is one of the finest coast-lines in all Britain.

Particularly interesting is the Lady's Window, a curious rock formation, 'a perforated rocky crag, sharply silhouetted against the sky.' Provided you have a head for heights you may be tempt-ed to step through the narrow - very narrow - ledge and look down some 200 feet to the sea. Trevethet Gutt too is a lovely creek, and like so much is probably best seen from a boat.

Perhaps, inevitably, any visit to this northern corner of Cornwall should end on the coast. This cliffscape, in moments of imagination, can become a theatre, the stage for something natu-ral or unnatural, or even supernatural; and the gulls with their acrobatics intensify the effect, their quick low 'qua-qua-qua' filling the land, the sea and the sky.

And don't be frightened by the weather - by what we foolishly call 'bad weather.' The truth is each day brings a different image, a fresh experience.

A LAST WORD

YOU cannot do Boscastle in a day or a week - or even a life- time. Boscastle, at its best, and the surrounding district are a renewing, ongoing experience. Thomas Burke once said of Tintagel: 'What it has to give must be received individually. . .' That applies to Boscastle too.

The strange fact is this whole stretch of North Cornwall is a feeling as much as a location on the map of Cornwall. There is an indefinable something here: a kind of magic.

Perhaps we should go to the gifted Ronald Duncan for a few last thoughts. Standing on cliffs, to the north of Boscastle, years ago he told an aspiring publisher: 'These cliffs, they seem to despise and defy humanity . . . and the gales we get along this coast make a comment with which I agree.'

Boscastle Harbour   C.A.Vincent

45

MORE BOSSINEY BOOKS . . .

TINTAGEL
Michael Williams

KING ARTHUR COUNTRY
Brenda Duxbury, Michael Williams & Colin Wilson

LEGENDS OF CORNWALL
Sally Jones

GHOSTS OF CORNWALL
Peter Underwood

CORNWALL — LAND OF LEGEND
Joy Wilson

WESTCOUNTRY MYSTERIES
Introduced by Colin Wilson

DISCOVERING BODMIN MOOR
E.V. Thompson

THE CRUEL CORNISH SEA
David Mudd

LOCATION — CORNWALL
David Clarke

HIDDEN KNOWLEDGE
Lori Reid

SAINTS OF THE SOUTH WEST
James Mildren

CASTLES OF CORNWALL
Mary & Hal Price

We shall be pleased to send you our catalogue giving full details of our growing list of titles for Devon, Cornwall, Dorset, Wiltshire and Somerset as well as forthcoming publications. If you have difficulty in obtaining our titles, write direct to Bossiney Books, Land's End, St Teath, Bodmin, Cornwall.